2024

VIRGO HOROSCOPES

Astrid Luna

PUBLISHED BY:
SHAKTI Copyright © 2012

2024 Astrology

Open mindedness is key for a good romantic life during 2024. In career persistence is key for success, as success comes at unlikely times and in unlikely ways. Self care and confronting challenges will help confidence and feeling full of vitality.

To maintain good health throughout 2024, prioritize self-care and follow a healthy diet and exercise routine. By seizing the positive energies of the year and confronting challenges head-on, this could be a year of transformation and personal fulfillment for everyone.

Optimism and a feeling of freedom enters with the entry of Sagittarius into Venus. We may even find ourselves more open to romantic adventure. This is all beginning near the start of the year on the eighteenth of January so let´s start to enjoy.

With Aquarius being entered by Mercury on the twentieth of February we see our communication become more innovative and learning more progressive.

Mercury then retrogrades in Aries on th
second of April however so we are all
advised to be more cautious.

On the first of May Taurus is entered by
Jupiter, so our feelings of abundance
and expansion will be at an all time high.
Taurus associates with stability and

material possesions and sensuality, so we can expect to see these feelings especially in these areas. During this transit we may also see increased prosperity.

We may experience some delays or a sense of things slowing down during the retrograde of Saturn in Aquarius. This happens on the thirtieth of June and we may need to take time to reassess things and adjust. Remain determined.

With the Mercury retrograde in Leo on

the fifth of August we find ourselves

reassessing and reflecting and fining our

own leadership qualities and how to

express ourselves to the best of what we

feel we may be able to do.

On October the ninth there is a

retrograde in Taurus of Jupiter so it is

time to review our aspirations and adjust

to things.

There is another retrograde in November, on the twenty sixth, this time Mercury in Scorpio.

The retrograde of Mars in Cancer the first week of December makes us reevaluate our passions and desires.

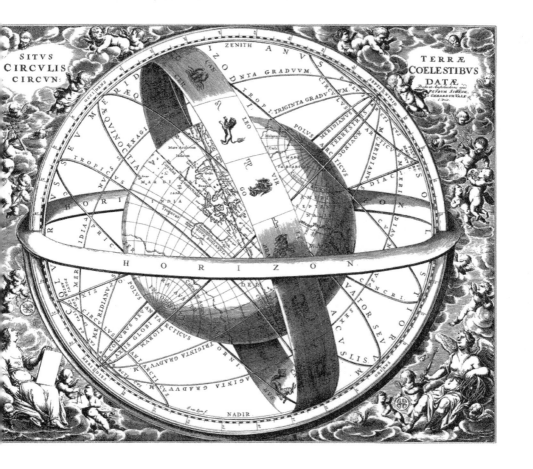

he Earth element rules Virgo , the planet

ercury and the sixth house. Both kind and

phisticated a Virgo will tend to persevere

lietly until the job is done. They are good at

eing the bigger picture and this makes them

amazing friends often able to lend a hand and give sound advise.

Virgos do have a deep inner world and at times, before confidence has been developed they may appear to be shy. Once the confidence and trust has been established however you will find you have a loyal friend usually for the long haul.

Although Virgo may seem shy, as an Earth
sign their sensual desires are strong and they
are in fact one of the most passionate signs.

They love to connect deeply with their partner

and celebrate this connection in the bedroom. Virgos do expect perfection, from themselves and others, and so may appear at times to be somewhat critical, yet this is simply because their standards are high. They hold themselves to high standards, and so also expect others to adhere to these.

Virgos love beauty and take good care of their appearance. They do strive for perfection and it brings them peace of mind. Their organisation keeps their life running smoothly and is an absolute necessity for a Virgo. They are always ready to try new things and keep learning.

he year 2024 may be the most

ignificant year for Virgos in the last ten

years. There is a sense of calm and security within all areas of life this year fo Virgos, as well as lots of transformation. The year begins with a bang.

2024 will be especially transformative in the area of emotions for Virgo, and there will be some truly special moments.

...s the area of romance has been

...omewhat neglected in recent times,

...irgos will find themselves focusing more

...n this area of their lives.

Transformative change comes with certa

planetary movements such as Jupiter, th

planet of optimism and expansion,

entering Pisces which is especially

favourable for Virgoan finanacial pursuits,

in fact we may see new streams of

income coming in with this planetary shift.

Mars also plays a significant role,

increasing your passion and drive, Virgo,

where you may find yourselves taking

advantage of more of the opportunities

coming your way and surmounting any

obstacles along your path.

You will at times feel unstoppable, Virgo.

www.onelifetemple.com